# Honorable Discharge
## 26 things every vet needs to know when giving up is all they think is left

### Preface and Special Thanks

*"I appreciate your determination in showing me I can do it! Thanking you for your perseverance, support, and love!"*

### Chapter 1

*"The past was always there, lived inside of you, and it helped make you who you were. But it had to be placed in perspective. The past could not dominate the future."*
*– Barbara Taylor Bradford,*

### Chapter 2

*"The purpose of life is to discover your gift. The meaning of life is to give your gift away."*
*-David Viscott*

### Chapter 3

*"I can assure you, public service is a stimulating, proud and lively enterprise. It is not just a way of life, it is a way to live fully.- Lee Hamilton*

### Chapter 4

*"Sometimes it's easy to walk by because we know we can't change someone's whole life in a single afternoon. But what we fail to realize it that simple*

*kindness can go a long way toward encouraging someone who is stuck in a desolate place."* -― **Mike Yankoski**

## Chapter 5

*"When you imitate others in real life, you deny the world benefits of your uniqueness. So be who you were born to be."* ― **Gift Gugu Mona**

## Chapter 6

*"Money is only a tool. It will take you wherever you wish, but it will not replace you as the driver."* —**Ayn Rand**

## Chapter 7

*"The best way to not feel hopeless is to get up and do something. Don't wait for good things to happen to you. If you go out and make some good things happen, you will fill the world with hope, you will fill yourself with hope."*

― **Barack Obama**

## Chapter 8

*"The truth is, unless you let go, unless you forgive yourself, unless you forgive the situation, unless you realize that the situation is over, you cannot move forward."*-- **Steve Maraboli**

# Preface and special thanks:

*"I appreciate your determination in showing me I can do it! Thanking you for your perseverance, support, and love!"*

Hello there and thank you for purchasing this book. Trust me when I tell you that this is an invaluable resource for veterans of the US military with some collateral benefits for people who are homeless and just need some assistance. I had no idea I would be writing about the topic outlined in this book ever but because of some personal struggles in 2018 I had to go through some very dark times to learn about myself and the VA system in order to share this information.

Where I am today is an amazing place both spiritual and financial but the most important thing is I am living my purpose.The light in me shines greater than ever before . I would be remiss if I didn't thank the people along the way who have helped me through this scary, fascinating, dark, painful, and incredible journey.

First off thank you to Paul, the support he provided me the entire step of the way not to mention he was the one who gave me the final push to start this journey. "Paul I know everything will turn out great for you as your purpose may have been to meet me"

Next, thank you to a wonderful person and a great friend who never left my side, Jodi. Jodi always spoke about authenticity and purpose yet I never listened Jodster I am listening now and I love you dearly. Jodi you have been super supportive the entire journey. Jodi has personally witnessed the fall of me from when I was doing really well living in the radius and enjoying my journey to the dark deep hole I fell into. Now the rebirth of me to get back to living my purpose and being my authentic self.

To my brother Mel and my stepfather Joe who kept me accountable, got me to rehab "again" and stayed helpful and nurturing when I didn't deserve the kindness extended. "Joe your promise to my mom is complete and you stepped up huge when literally no one else would"

Thank you to Muriam and Tracy for showing me the path that motivated me again and the beginning of how to navigate the VA system I really appreciate you guys. Thank you Tim and Mike for providing the idea and planting the seeds you guys motivated me through this process from the very start and ultimately assisting me hit the finish line so others can read this little guide going forward.

Thank you Prism for your wisdom and openmidedness.I love how you show up in life and can't imagine how you overcame so much with grace, kindness, and dignity. I love the fact that you're my friend, my mentor,  and one of my favorite confidants.

Thank you Stacy you have had some challenges being my friend.  I know we don't always see eye to eye. I am grateful for our connection that is undeniable and I am thankful that  you participate in my life you showed up for me when nobody else would and you listened when no one else could.Finally thank you to Rachel and Morgan for helping me hit the bottom. Once I hit bedrock the only way for me to go was up.

I once heard a quote, Don't forget 3 types of people in your life, Those who helped you in difficult times, those who left you in difficult times and those who put you in difficult times. All above mentioned fall into those categories and my gratitude is poised and never ending. When people show you who they are, believe them. How I got here and where I came from is quite a journey. I am here to share with you my journey and will show you how you can get back hope, love, and most importantly purpose,with some help from the VA and the organizations in your state get up off the mat and move on to the next phase of your life. I promise if you do the things I mention in this book you will help yourself quickly and be on a path to help others. It is my hope that every veteran utilizes the benefits afforded to them by the US government because I have found that so many don't use them and worse yet don't even know about the benefits available. So grab a highlighter or at least a pen and take some notes because the nuggets I have for you I have found and used myself. Again thank you and God Bless the USA! Enjoy!

## Chapter 1

*"The past was always there, lived inside of you, and it helped make you who you were. But it had to be placed in perspective. The past could not dominate the future."*
― **Barbara Taylor Bradford**,

This is a how to book for veterans who need a leg up. I have spent the past year going through what many veterans may go through at some point in their civilian lives, or at the very least something similar. Trust me when I tell you that I empathize and understand your situation. I personally was over $70,000 in debt to my creditors, broke, ( that means zero money, bad credit, no job)  cell phone turned off, 2 car payments behind,  2 months behind on rent, drinking excessively, and it all came to a head when I was passed out in my car ( that had no insurance on it ) in the parking lot of my ex girlfriend when the police took me into custody. I think you can agree this was the bottom. For at least a week I had thought nothing other than jumping off a tall building or getting 1000 mg of oxycontin and wash it down with a bottle of Johnny Walker.

It was at this time that my last remaining immediate family member, my brother Mike was ready to do one last thing for me and that was to send me off to rehab for the 3rd time. I had a week to figure out how to get to rehab.

I concluded that I was fortunate in that I knew a couple people in the drug/alcohol community and subsequently reached out to them. First off I had an old friend, Jason ( I have known Jason almost 20yrs) who with the help of his father has built a wonderful community of recovery including, In Patient, outpatient, and county jail treatment facilities with sober housing, once complete with treatment his sober community provides patents with job opportunities, and a safe place for people to go post treatment. I spoke with Jason, he told me that even though he had room for me he would not take me due to conflict of interest. Jason has long since been removed from the day to day operations. Strike one.

I was thinking, "ok I will call an old friend whom I had actually partied with in my younger days and subsequently ran into him later in the recovery rooms in the early 2000's. Tom (I have known Tom for 30 years!) he oversees the treatment program at the Salvation Army. I placed a call to Tom and he either never received the message or decided to never call me back. ( still waiting for you Tom) These are 2 prime examples of why I left the recovery/AA community 5 years prior. My experience had been one of people acting one way in the rooms and behaving another way in their personal and professional lives at the very least, at the most, they, like many others, gave up on me.

I was hatching my plan to commit suicide ( I still have it in my google drive as a reminder ) I contacted my friend from Arizona ( Paul) who simply said to me, " aren't you a vet?" to which I said, "yes." He advised me of a program that would help me sober up and get my life back to some semblance of normalcy. I had no idea what I was in for. The lessons, information, and benefits offered to basically any honorably discharged veteran I discovered have been nothing short of a miracle , so much so that I had to put it on paper so any veteran who feels like they are out of options can find that there are options out there. ( there is also information in this book for those who are not vets as well ) No matter how far down the rabbit hole you think you are, if you want your life back, I am going to show you the path. I have learned of many benefits and utilized them all. All of this can be accomplished this inside of 1 year! If you are ready to get started, I will show you my starting point and if you do the things I outline in the chapters ahead, I know that you too will get your life back, and your life will transform into what you always thought it could be many days/years ago.

First I need to give you some backstory. I want veterans to understand that anyone can accomplish making a comeback when you learn about me. I never thought I would ever be talking about my military service because I didn't have a very good expirence.My military experience was one of shame, alcoholism, and general disdain. I have never been a normal person. I don't like rules, ( although I can conform for a specific set amount of time) working for someone else has always been a chore for me. I am an entrepreneur. I have sold recreational pharmaceuticals, ran underground poker games, sold through an online website, hosted events, worked in outside sales, and now I enjoy writing.  My youth was spent  as an outgoing, run of the mill kid. I played sports including golf and basketball neither of which I was really good at,  I was average. I performed in theatre which I could not carry a note for the performances with a suitcase. I was a below average student because school wasn't something I enjoyed. (2.0 GPA) . I was the kid who went to and thru the keg parties when the parents were out of town. I chased girls, and generally goofed off. Finally it was time for me to start thinking about what to do after high school, I didnt think about it.  I figured  my parents would  send me off to college just like my friends parents did.  I would find my calling and purpose once there...that, did not happen. My father in his infinite wisdom or unbelievable selfishness told me that if I went to college on my own accord and achieved a GPA of over 3.0 he would be happy to reimburse me for my schooling upon graduation.

Here is the thing, back in the late 80's and early 90's a teenager getting student loans without parental assistance wasn't happening. The federal government wasn't passing out student loans like they do now in the 2019's. As of 2019 the student debt is over 1 trillion dollars. Let's tell it like it is, college wasn't really an option for me. If I worked while in school and studied hard, a 3.0 GPA might not be attainable. The year after high school I worked two jobs, lived in an apartment with a couple friends working mundane low paying jobs. I soon discovered that most of my friends had gone off to college and only returned for the holidays. I was already being left behind. I asked my father for a piece of advice. I asked him if he would change his mind about paying for a year of college to see if I could do it. He said "no." My father instead gave me the best piece of advice he could at the time, he said, " You know your uncle ( his brother) went into the military and that turned him around". I had no idea my father thought I needed my life to be turned around. I was 19 yrs old, never in trouble, I was mostly confused as any 19yr old is.

I took in my father's advice. A month later I went on a road trip to North Carolina to visit another friend. My friend Mike was in the Army, stationed at Ft. Bragg in the

82st airborne, he absolutely loved it! Mike was a police officer and a paratrooper. I came home to Minnesota and promptly joined the Army. My occupation, radio operator. I was excited and terrified all at the same time. Let the journey begin.          I entered into the military on April 4 1989 off to South Carolina,  Ft Jackson. Eight weeks of basic training and learning what it is like to be a soldier. I quickly learned that the people who joined the enlisted ranks weren't the most educated people I had ever met. What was surprising to me was that most of the guys were from poorer areas of their respective states which astonished me. I guess I figured the men would be more like me ( just a little confused and or motivated to get some college money)  I learned about many things I knew nothing about, including a new vernacular, grits, southern slang, and special modifications to automobiles.  I assimilated accordingly at least for the most part anyway. Shooting a M16, marching, camping in the woods, and military training wasn't for me. I figured eight weeks wasn't that much to deal with and then I would soon be doing my job, spending time with men who were similar to me and learning about how the telecommunications world worked. I finished basic training with  a couple hiccups as my bunkmate was the platoon laggard and I got into a fight with another guy over disrespect. All in all basic training wasn't that hard but I was glad when it ended. Off to my job training at Ft Gordon Georgia where I started to learn how to be a radio operator. I was really enjoying it when I was told that because I smoked marijuana as a teenager I was a security risk and couldn't work the job of radio operator ( 31 C) anymore. It was on THIS day that I had to choose what my NEW occupation was to be. Nineteen years old and I had to make this choice without any of my support group, I choose electrician, why? I don't know. I was promptly put on a plane to Ft Leonard Wood MO and this is where my disdain for the Army began.

I got off the plane in Missouri at 2 in the morning picked up by an army soldier from Ft Leonard Wood and off to my new platoon. 3 in the morning and a drill sergeant looks at me. My uniform was a little disheveled, hence I was doing push ups and running to HIS heart's content in the middle of the fucking night. I stayed in MO for another eight weeks learning the basics about being an electrician then I learned where my first duty station would be, Ft Wainwright AK.

Alaska is a beautiful state, five times the size of Texas, mountains and truly a hunter and fishermans paradise. Most Minnesota men would love Alaska, this Minnesotan by way of Illinois man did not enjoy it one little bit. I was never a fan of hunting or fishing and I despise cold weather. Fairbanks Alaska has some harsh weather in the summer as well as the winter. Also, in case you didn't know, three months of the year its daylight all day everyday. Upon my arrival to "the last frontier state" I was greeted by my military unit and promptly hazed. I was beaten, stripped, hogtied and had a mop up my ass and left in the mop closet for about 12 hours. I can still to this day name all the culprits in case one of them happens to read this book one day. After 2 years in Alaska I was done. Former US President George Bush ended the war with Iraq, the first war with Iraq. President Bush told the troops if they wanted out of the US Army they could get an honorable discharge. Upon hearing that I was ready to go home. I told you that little story to advise you that I am a qualified veteran?

While I was in the US Army I developed quite the alcohol addiction. The nightmares from the first week in Alaska haunt me to this day. I went back to Minnesota after discharge from the US Army. Twenty five years later, 3 inpatient treatments hundreds of thousands of dollars, 1 failed marriage, 3 failed relationships, an adopted child, deaths of both parents, the death of my closest friend, It was time to die. God had another plan for me...

## Chapter 2
*"The purpose of life is to discover your gift. The meaning of life is to give your gift away."*
**-David Viscott**

I have tried many occupations for a hot minute and discovered that I am rather average at many different things but not great at any of them, moreover I have discovered that the most important thing in a man's life is his purpose. ***This is the first thing that I recommend you search for.*** Look inside yourself and ask yourself this question, "What is it I do for no money? What is it I love doing all the time even when I didn't have any money. The thing I have found is that when we discover what our purpose is, any addictive behaviors seem to subside. It doesn't matter what our purpose is and it for many people (myself included) is often overlooked or lost in the busy thing we call life. We get into romantic relationships, start families, need money for the things we want and for everyday living. Somewhere along the way we either forget our purpose or no longer have time to cultivate it. I encourage everyone reading this booklet to look deep inside yourself everyday for at least 15 minutes and think HARD about this. "What do I love doing and would still do even when I make no money at it but enjoy it thoroughly ?"

Everyone and I mean everyone has something that they love to do and do it better than their family friends and most other people. If you figure this out, trust me when I tell you that there is a way to make a living doing it. That will be the last day you every WORK for the rest of your life because you will be doing what you love doing and living your purpose. Your food will taste better, you will embrace strangers,you will sleep better, and you will find yourself inexplicably happy. I have always enjoyed writing, I am a good storyteller, and love helping others. That is why I am writing this little booklet. God willing, it will be here long after I am gone and my hope is that it will help others on their journey not only navigating the VA but finding their purpose along the way thus discovering true happiness. My parents never taught me about purpose I don't blame them for that as I don't think they ever lived their purpose hence my parents look happy on the outside yet are very angry stressed out people. It wasn't until I was in my mid forties and utilizing a life coach, broke, in rehab, homeless, subject to a phycologist, psychiatrist, and counselors that this became abundantly clear. I always thought money, the right partner, the right neighborhood, or the right friends would make me happy. I would wake up in the morning and I never was thinking about my purpose I was always thinking about how I needed more money, needed the right partner, or to have the right friends etc. I stopped caring about all that and my life started to take some interesting changes, again it started with my brother taking me to rehab.

Family is an important thing in almost all peoples lives. A wise man once told me that the family you are born into ISNT the family you die with. I say this because I was estranged from my original family for many years and now

I dont have the chance to make that right. Its ok, the family I die with will be grateful for the time they spend with me going forward. My father was never around for me and my parents divorced when I was a teenager. Growing up is hard for everyone I am not going to minimize other people's story mine was what it was and for me I spent most of my time navigating and figuring stuff out on my own. This is another reason I am writing this how to book as my natural curiosity has granted me many insights that most readers I hope will appreciate in the coming chapters. My travels have taken me many places and I have quite a story to tell, but this is a how to book and if you care to read my story you can find it at www.*bearjay99.com* - check out the blog to read how my story began and has unfolded thus far..

All through my travels alcohol has been a mainstay, either drinking it (usually to excess) or maintaining sobriety which is where I am at as of this books printing. I tried the AA thing and after 9 years I found it wasn't for me. I also discovered that drinking isn't my problem, drinking is my solution to my problems. When I am living my purpose I don't find a reason to drink and thus I don't drink to excess. Just to qualify though I do have many DWI's, many lost relationships, and many run ins with the police due to being intoxicated. I behaved very poorly on the job and showed up terrible in my romantic and familial relationships due to excessive use of the substance alcohol, some would definitely say alcoholism. There is alcoholism in my family or origin and drinking is an integral part of all family functions. Maybe it is due to my irish heritage or maybe it is because it is easier to deal with family functions properly lubricated. I don't think to much about the next time comes that I will drink alcohol but I know I don't have to drink today. I am super grateful that I found the VA hospital in my darkest hour.It is absolutely awesome the programs available to me as a veteran. In the next few chapters I will disclose what I have learned so others can take advantage of the programs and benefits available to every veteran in the USA. My hope is that like me they get to the place where drinking or using drugs isn't the only option. The reader will discover that there are so many options available. This is why it is true that living in the USA is the only place I ever want to live. God Bless the USA!

## Chapter 3

*I can assure you, public service is a stimulating, proud and lively enterprise. It is not just a way of life, it is a way to live fully.-* **Lee Hamilton**

There are as of this printing about 20 million veterans in the USA that is about 6% of the total population. Half of all veterans are served by the Department of Veterans

Affairs. 90% of all veterans are male and the majority of veterans are from the gulf war era ( 53%). A pew survey done in 2017 found that the least favorable government program is the VA, however 75% of the US population supports increased spending in the VA over all other government program spending. In order to receive benefits from the VA one would have to have served in the US military and was discharged honorably for a period greater than 2 years.

One of the reasons I am writing this is because my stepfather (Joe) who is 65 yrs old and qualifies for VA health care didnt even know the breadth and width of services available to him after he lost his government job due to city politics and subsequently lost his health care. We will get to his benefits later in this how to book.

The United States Department of Veterans Affairs (**VA**) is a federal agency. The agency provides comprehensive  services to eligible military veterans at VA medical centers as well as  outpatient clinics located throughout the United States including  several non-healthcare benefits plus disability compensation, vocational rehabilitation, education assistance, home loans, and life insurance; and provides burial and memorial benefits to veterans and family members at 135 national cemeteries.

I will start at my beginning including my personal experience and also contribute everything I found out as it relates to the VA and all the benefits. If you are a veteran and struggle with addiction, substance abuse or any of a multitude of mental health challenges as many veterans do. ( 56% of all vets struggle with PTSD, depression and/or addiction/substance abuse ) The VA has a wonderful program referred to as RRTP ( Residential Rehabilitation Treatment Program) *I love how the government always uses acronyms for everything.* The program is tailored to the veterans needs including: alcoholism, drug addiction, all forms including opioid, weight, and gambling. Sex trauma and PTSD are also on the menu. The stay in RRTP will be anywhere from 30 to 90 days. The veteran will go through recreational therapy, mindfulness, anger management, counselling, psychotherapy, and meditation. The hospital is completely staffed with all medical professionals and has all the amenities to start the process in getting guys back on track with their life. I personally have been though a few programs and this one is amazing! This program in the civilian world doesn't exist and if it did it would cost in excess of $50k. Most insurance companies won't let anyone go to a treatment program like this for longer than 28 days.

   After the veteran leaves the RRTP inpatient program they head off to the outpatient and or aftercare ( 3 to 6 months) . This is where the benefits start getting fantastic and every veteran is entitled to them. After the smart recovery program is complete and the veteran is homeless, will be homeless, or would be going back to an unsafe environment. The veteran can go to the VA hospital and stay on the grounds in shared hospital type setting for up to 2 years. The housing is 2 man rooms, they are complete with all amenities including a community kitchen, community living area, high speed internet, and satellite television while they go through the process of treatment and transition to permanent safe housing, ie; regular life again.

While at the hospital, the veteran has access to all the same benefits that they received in the inpatient program as well as many others like clothing. A veteran can get boots, shoes, t-shirts, underwear, socks, sweatshirts, jackets, thermal underwear, gloves and stocking cap all for no cost. One of the places the veteran can go is a place called Stand down. Stand down is the program where people donate the aforementioned items. Also, the US government donates items that are unused! Later in the process the veteran can get suits, ties and dress shoes to interview for that job to get back on their career path. The clothing doesn't stop there either because if the veteran does side work they can get specialized clothing as well. So for review, all clothing the veteran can procure is,

1. **Basic needs clothing:** t-shirts, jeans, boots, tennis shoes, socks, underwear etc
2. **Interview clothing** : Suits ties, dress shoes, belt or suspenders

3. **Outerwear**, boots, gloves, stocking caps, jacket(s)
4. **Active wear or specialized wear for work**: tennis shoes, specific uniforms

Next we are going to mention toiletries and healthcare products? TheVA gets many donations of said items from hotels and people who support veterans including: shampoo, conditioner, toothpaste, toothbrushes, floss, soap, shaving cream, razors, aftershave, hair gel, nail clippers, lotion, and cotton swabs, you get the idea. All for free as long as the veteran stays in the program and is making positive progress. Haircut anyone? There are a few barbershops and salons that will cut a veterans hair for free. ( voucher from hospital or donating organization)

Think about what we have already discovered, 50k for inpatient treatment. Basic needs like clothing and housing, (complete with all the comforts of home) and toiletries that for 1 person might cost about $100 a month all for the price of helping oneself.

Now we have gone through shelter, clothing, and toiletries wait, there's more. If the veteran is service connected ( I will get into service connection later ) transportation is free as well. Public transportation in the state of MN ( check your state to see if it is available in yours as well)  is free to all veterans. The veteran simply has to get on any public transportation and show them your veterans ID card. After the veteran has been in the program and making progress they are free to go find some employment, actually it is recommended and encouraged. The resources for employment are also fantastic. If the veteran has a skill but no resume they can go the work center at the VA and take classes on how to create a resume.

Then, once the resume has been created, I personally recommend setting up a LinkedIn ( www.linkedin.com) account in order to help you get found by various recruiters and search for jobs. All veterans get priority on USA jobs. ( www.usajobs.com) Next, put the resume on the websites available to you including Indeed ( www.indeed.com) and Monster (www.Monster.com)as well . Further the VA in coordination with the workforce center will help with job interviewing skills. Many people struggle with interviewing and subsequently struggle and might give up on that crucial part of the job hunting processes, so they get hired. There are job boards that cater to veterans specifically to veterans including jobs for vets ( www.jobsforvets.com)and usajobs (www.usajobs.com) There is also an opportunity for the veteran needs to get some new skills or some updating of skills? Schooling is available to veterans free of charge as well . A veteran can utilize their GI bill for schooling, or the VA has programs available if the veteran is service connected to go all the way to a PHD (*provided they keep their grades up*) to get the veteran back in the workforce. These programs are all available at no charge.

Also there are other ways for the veteran to earn money while in the program and investigating tirelessly their purpose all the while waiting on the government bureaucracy for the paperwork ( service connection and housing ) to be completed. In the VA Hospital many Universities and research organizations are actively doing studies on veterans for the various ailments that brought them into the VA to begin with. The studies can be a one off for $50 or $100 or the studies can be longer and can up to a couple thousand dollars. Another way to make money while in the program is simple job boards like craigslist where a veteran can work an event or do some work for a person or organization for a weekend or a day in order to make a few hundred dollars. I personally even donated plasma and sperm so check your area regarding both of those options. A person can make over 2000 a month donating alone. Another thing a few veterans have done is medical studies and focus groups there are quite a bit of criteria associated with both of those options but you just never know what you might qualify for and the time to do stuff like this is when you are in a setting like treatment.

## Chapter 4

*"Sometimes it's easy to walk by because we know we can't change someone's whole life in a single afternoon. But what we fail to realize it that simple kindness can go a long way toward encouraging*

*someone who is stuck in a desolate place."*   *-— Mike Yankoski*

Homelessness is truly a tragic thing. In the wealthiest country in the world there is zero excuse for anyone to be living on the street. Most people believe it is because of circumstances mostly by the individual but that isn't always the case. In 2018 a study discovered that 38,000 veterans were homeless. Of all adults in the US 9% of them are veterans. The US government made a commitment to end veteran homelessness in the US in 2014. Subsequently it is being overcome slowly but surely. The biggest hurdle I have noticed is related to a couple things as it relates to the veteran.

- <u>Motivation</u> - the world is an ever changing place and I have noticed that some just aren't motivated to change with the tides and thus give up.
- <u>Self Esteem</u>- I have found that when life kicks some people in the ass one to many times the self talk gets to be brutal on oneself
- <u>Mental Health</u>- Many people who are homeless don't have the ability to get the care needed to help with their mental health needs and subsequently a lot of the times self medication ( alcohol and drugs) becomes the solution.

One of the programs that is out there and a little unknown is the Grant Per Diem program. It is a program for homeless veterans that will take them in from prison or mental health facilities and provide the veteran with food, shelter, and clothing including the resources to get on their feet and the process can last as long as 2 years. Another program out there is : Common Bond --Subsidized housing CRRC -- The Community Resource Center is available to Veterans for things like showers, food, laundry, and toiletries. The CRRC is also a place for veterans to receive services including referrals for treatment, housing, shelter, etc. The CRRC is a wonderful starting point for a veteran who is in need of various assistance.

Veterans specifically can benefit from many of these programs if only they were more informed. The thing is, the US government isn't going to start a marketing campaign to let veterans know that they are entitled to money and assistance. In the case of my stepfather who mind you is 65 yrs old. He thought he was entitled to a burial site and an emotional assistance dog. What he discovered and any vet can as well is something called service connection.

Service Connection is a program created for veterans who had any type of medically related problem that occured in the Armed Forces. The rating system is a percentage scale in 10 percent increments.  For example say you were a tank mechanic in the Army and were around loud noises your entire tour of duty. Maybe you had some hearing loss. This is one example of service connection I can offer you. I will also tell you that the veteran can submit the appropriate paperwork to the Veterans Affairs Hospital and see if they qualify for service connection. It is in the best interest of the veteran to use a "sponsor" such as the American Legion or VSO. In order to do this it is important to submit an intent to file first so if the veteran gets awarded any service connection payment goes all the way back to the intent to file date. Keep in mind that the Veterans Affairs Hospital system generally refuses most claims the first time, so it is advised to continue to try until the claim is either accepted or the veteran has exhausted all appeals. Also know that this process can take years so get ready for the long haul.

Once the veteran is service connected they are allowed to take all public transportation at no cost to them. The next couple benefits most veterans have heard about and that is the GI Bill for college also there is the use of a service dog for emotional support which some people as they age get a little lonely and a companion is just the ticket to a better quality of life. Every soldier is entitled to a death benefit at no cost to them so the veteran can have a proper burial. It is important to go through the ever important benefits that every veteran can get depending on your state the benefits can be even greater.

## Chapter 5

*you imitate others in real life, you deny the ...nefits of your uniqueness. So be who you were ...to be.*" — **Gift Gugu Mona**

If you served in the United States Armed Forces for at least 24 months and received an honorable discharge the programs out there are absolutely amazing and here is where we are going to dive straight into them. You can also visit my Youtube channel for updates regularly for specific state veteran information because the assistance might vary from state to state.. So here we go, for starters :

- **Service Connection** - Any disability that a veteran has that can be traced back to the veterans time in the armed forces. Visit the local VSO for necessary steps to get paperwork submitted. Also have DD214 handy
- **Health Care** - The VA Hospital system which consists of over 1000 hospitals nationwide will provide comprehensive health care for all based on financial ability and care needs
- **Dental Care**- Veteran can get dental care at the VA. Also in some states there is a grant the veteran can get in order to do more dental services ( MN is one such state)
- **Eyewear** - Again in some states veterans can get annual eyewear from approved government vendors ( MN the voucher is for $400)

- **Acupuncture-** Traditional methods are not the only type of care   The Mental Health unit will provide meals for vets with immediate mental health needs.
- **Food Benefits** -Veterans who have financial struggles can qualify for SNAP benefits that can be applied for at the county office- and the VA provides vouchers
- **Cell Phone** - Once the veteran can prove they are on SNAP benefits they can get a government issued cell phone ( service is free but phone costs $40)
- **Bankruptcy-** If the veteran has financial needs that can be afforded a bankruptcy attorney can be appointed to help with that.
- **Criminal Court** - If the veteran has pending criminal charges they can choose veterans court where veterans can go and work through the criminal charges with less long lasting impact
- **Identification-** Veterans can go to a local outlet to receive a voucher in order to get an ID card for various needs

    SSN- Veteran can go to the local office to get a social security card in order to get employment with an ID card
- **Resume assistance-** Veteran can get help with **LinkedIn** and **Indeed**  so with the

*"When you imitate others in real life, you deny the world benefits of your uniqueness. So be who you were born to be."* – **Gift Gugu Mona**

If you served in the United States Armed Forces for at least 24 months and received an honorable discharge the programs out there are absolutely amazing and here is where we are going to dive straight into them. You can also visit my Youtube channel for updates regularly for specific state veteran information because the assistance might vary from state to state.. So here we go, for starters :

- **Service Connection** - Any disability that a veteran has that can be traced back to the veterans time in the armed forces. Visit the local VSO for necessary steps to get paperwork submitted. Also have DD214 handy
- **Health Care** - The VA Hospital system which consists of over 1000 hospitals nationwide will provide comprehensive health care for all based on financial ability and care needs
- **Dental Care**- Veteran can get dental care at the VA. Also in some states there is a grant the veteran can get in order to do more dental services ( MN is one such state)
- **Eyewear** - Again in some states veterans can get annual eyewear from approved government vendors ( MN the voucher is for $400)

- **Acupuncture-** Traditional methods are not the only type of care    The Mental Health unit will provide meals for vets with immediate mental health needs.
- **Food Benefits** -Veterans who have financial struggles can qualify for SNAP benefits that can be applied for at the county office- and the VA provides vouchers
- **Cell Phone** - Once the veteran can prove they are on SNAP benefits they can get a government issued cell phone ( service is free but phone costs $40)
- **Bankruptcy-** If the veteran has financial needs that can be afforded a bankruptcy attorney can be appointed to help with that.
- **Criminal Court** - If the veteran has pending criminal charges they can choose veterans court where veterans can go and work through the criminal charges with less long lasting impact
- **Identification-** Veterans can go to a local outlet to receive a voucher in order to get an ID card for various needs
    - SSN- Veteran can go to the local office to get a social security card in order to get employment with an ID card
- **Resume assistance-** Veteran can get help with **LinkedIn** and **Indeed**  so with the

aforementioned items they can get gainful employment and navigate back into the community

- **VA Employment** - When the veteran is in the GPD program they can work at the hospital in a work therapy capacity where they can acquire skills to get back into the workforce while they spice up their resume
- **Clothing** - The veteran can connect with organizations that provide interview clothing including suits and accessories for the perfect presentation outfit/ clothing for
- **Housing -** Once the veteran has completed a program for rehabilitation or was homeless, or coming out of a penal facility the VA has transitional housing available until they go into permanent housing whether it be on federal land or in the community. ( income permitting) further there are organizations that will help with first month and security deposit for the veteran
- **Furniture-** Once a place has been secured there are organizations that will help furnish the apartment ( in MN its called bridging check your state for these type of organizations)
- **Transportation** - Veterans in the state of MN and many other states can ride free transportation

- **Fishing and Hunting License**- need a license to get your meditation on? Well yes veterans can get these as well no charge
- **Professional Sporting tickets**- if a veteran goes to www.vetticks.com they can sign up for free tickets to all their favorite sports teams
- **Theatre Tickets** -again vetticks.com
- **One time VA Loan** - The Va will provide any vet a one time loan up to $5000

The long and the short of it is, if you are veteran in the state of MN there is absolutely no reason you should be homeless. The opportunities for veterans are plentiful. If you want your life back and are willing to put in the work obtaining your life back it can happen inside of 1 year.

## Chapter 6

*"Money is only a tool. It will take you wherever you wish, but it will not replace you as the driver."* —**Ayn Rand**

While being in transition from being homeless to being self sufficient there is a process that needs to be started. While the veteran is working on so many things to get life turned around it is necessary to start the process of getting money so the veteran isn't fundless for when a permanent residence is found. The following list is some ideas about getting money quickly to be able to get started and it's not that hard to go out and make a little money to tie you over until everything else is in order. Here are some of the things you can do to make a few dollars in the short term.

- **Donate Plasma** - if you don't have hepatitis C or HIV you can donate plasma the plasma center will let you donate 2 times a week for a total of 8 times a month and you can make as much as $500 in 1 month
- **Donate Sperm**- If you are under the age of 40 you might be able to donate your sperm ( I know it sounds funny but the pay isn't funny) You can make another $1000 a month doing what comes ( no pun intended) naturally
- **Medical Studies** - There are drug companies that are always doing late stage human trials and the pay is as much as $9000 for a trial
- **Brand Ambassador Gig**- Food and Beverage companies travel the country handing out samples to people at various events and the pay is generally around $20 an hour ( might need bank account set up ) www.Craigslist.org/ Gigs
- **General Labor Gigs**- People are always looking for help with moving items and lawn care as well as other various duties. Again check www.Craigslist.org
- **Internet Surveys** - It is possible to make money from the hospital by doing surveys and medical

studies there are plenty of places online to do said surveys

- **Focus Groups** - You can do focus groups by signing up for them at www.focusgroups.org and you receive messages about participating and qualifications ( generally $50-$200 per)

## Chapter 7

*"The best way to not feel hopeless is to get up and do something. Don't wait for good things to happen to you. If you go out and make some good things happen, you will fill the world with hope, you will fill yourself with hope."*
— **Barack Obama**

The last year prior to writing this was an unbelievable struggle. Overcoming challenges is what makes life worth living. I had no idea of what was available to me as a veteran so I needed to share this, it is only the beginning. I have shared many ways for a veteran to "start over" and take advantage of the vast amount of programs available to each and every one of them. Everything I mentioned in this booklet I have personally done. What I discovered along the way is that the most fulfilling part of this journey was the people I met along the way, those put in front of me that I could help. I was in need of reconnecting with life. For me and maybe for those reading this it is important to remember that the key to a fulfilled life is balance, how I have noticed is to achieve that I must get out of myself and help others ( which is why this how to book came to fruition in the first place) If we set out to help others every day the world would be a far better place. I like to talk about this side of things because I have found that while searching for my own purpose that I have been given so much by way of people, friendships, and more importantly by way of knowledge. I have been amazed more each day by the amount of information I have received in this area for the veterans of this country and if we just help each other there is nothing we can't accomplish. Helping my fellow man is in this man's opinion what we were put on this earth for. I have learned a lot about purpose and fulfillment these days and those who work in the capacity of helping others seem to live more fulfilling lives.

## Chapter 8

*"The truth is, unless you let go, unless you forgive yourself, unless you forgive the situation, unless you realize that the situation is over, you cannot move forward."*-- **Steve Maraboli**

No matter how far down the scale we have gone, we learned that our experience can help others- one of my favorite quotes. Reconnecting with the world will take time but it will happen. I have personally learned that the world doesn't meet you halfway. I have also learned that there are people in your corner no matter how far down you have fallen. I mentioned earlier it is important to remember those who left you during difficult times, those who showed up for you during difficult times, and those who put you in difficult times. The first group we reconnect with is our family. I will advise you that the family you were born into isn't necessarily the family you will die with, I am always cognizant of that. Your family was probably the last to leave you and most likely will be the first to return to you. If you show up in your life and be your authentic self your family will be there for you and will want to help. Friends are another part of the new life for the veteran. The old friends might not be the best fit for the veteran especially if they are in a housing situation that is toxic. I encourage you to stick with those who have been there and those who have shown up during this difficult time in your life. When a person starts doing different and healthy things the people who are supposed to show up in life, will. This has been very true in my life, when I became open to the possibilities I discovered many but not all benefits for veterans and had to share them, along with a message of hope to all those who are reading this handbook.

When the veteran has accomplished the tasks set forth in this booklet it is time to go out there and live your purpose. If your purpose is that of a bartender, minister, husband, or writer. This is your life go out there and get going. The items in this book have shown a veteran how to go literally from the street all the way back to living in housing and working in a role to contribute to their community as they move towards their purpose in life.

So there it is, I can tell you from my personal experience that a mere 12 months ago I was alone, hopeless, jobless, penniless, and no roof over my head with my car repossessed. Today I have a host of friends new and old. My family is in a better place as it relates to me. I have found purpose and hope, not to mention love for myself as well as others. I am going to my new job, have a couple bucks in my pocket, I am starting over without any debt or consequences hanging over my head. I am looking for a new place to live. I hope this little booklet is a platform for others to learn from and gather some strength as they go on their path to purpose and a new life. Good Luck and god bless.